Final Wishes Planner:

Crafting Your Vigil and Memorial Options

Glenda Walsh Crouse, CEOLD

This is not a legally binding document. It is meant to plan and express your final wishes regarding your vigil, disposition, funeral and memorial services. This booklet does not include medical preferences and distribution of your assets. Keep this document in a safe place that can be easily accessible by trusted family and friends. You have permission to photocopy **completed** pages of this document to distribute to family and friends to notify them of your final wishes. If you would like assistance in completing this booklet contact me through my website. Additional end of life planning resources also available on the website.

www.glendawalshcrouse.com

Table of Contents

My Personal Contact Information & Details

Information in the section helps a family member or friend complete your obituary. Also, to post notice of your passing on your social media accounts; if you so desire. It also provides personal information that may be needed to complete other legal documents.

My Legal Name:

____

____

Maiden Name: ____

Nickname(s):____

Date of Birth: ____

Place of Birth: ____

Address:____

____

____

____

Home Phone:____

Cell Phone:____

Email address(es)/password(s):

____

____

____

____

Social media logins/passwords:

____

____

____

____

Other:____

____

____

____

____

Occupation:____

____

____

____

____

Citizenship(s):____

Military Service:

____

____

____

____

Education:____

____

____

____

____

Religious/ Spiritual Organizations:

____

____

____

____

Memberships in the following clubs/organizations:

____

____

____

____

Some of my favorite things:

____

____

____

____

____

____

A favorite memory:

____

____

____

____

____

____

____

____

Other Information:

<u>My Family Information</u>

Marital Status:____

Partner/ Spouse's Name: ____

Wedding Date: ____

My children, their partners/spouses and their children:

____

____

____

____

____

____

____

____

____

____

____

____

____

____

____

____

____

____

____

____

My siblings, their partners/spouses and their children:

My Father's Name:____

Father's Birthplace: ____

My Mother's

Name:____

Mother's Madien Name:____

Mother's Birthplace:____

Former Partner/ Spouse:

Other family members and their information:

<u>My Vigil Plan</u>

Person(s) who will oversee my vigil to make sure my wishes are honored and their contact information:

____

____

____

____

____

Vigil location:

____

____

____

____

____

If inside, windows open or closed? _______________________________

____

____

Would you like to rest in bed, a favorite chair/sofa, etc. Lying down, sitting up?

____

____

____

Who would you like to be present and their contact information:

____

____

____

____

Guests continued:

____
____
____
____
____
____
____
____
____
____
____
____
____
____
____
____
____
____
____
____
____

Pets who may attend:

____
____
____
____

People who I don't want to attend:

____

____

____

____

____

____

Medical Personnel to attend/ be on call for consultation and their contact information:

____

____

____

____

____

____

Medical needs, wants and information:

____

____

____

____

____

____

____

____

____

____

____

Allergies:

____

____

____

Where should visitors wait while waiting to see you?

____

____

____

Should we make a sign explaining your wishes to visitors who are waiting?

____

____

____

____

____

How should visitors enter your space?

____

____

____

How many people may visit at a time?

____

____

____

Would you like visitors to write in a journal during the visitation? This journal will become a keepsake for your family.

____

____

Would you like visitors to recall memories, share blessings, read letters, or bring an object to place on the altar/sacred space?

How long should visits last?

Lighting preferences:

Temperature preferences:

What do you want to wear?

Sounds:

Scent preferences:

Scents that are not welcome:

Music to be played:

Music that should not be played:

Music that should not be played continued:

Things to look at (artwork, photo albums visuals that are comforting):

Do you want an alter or spiritual/religious focal point? Items needed for this area:

Other items wanted in the location:

____

____

____

____

____

____

Room arrangement:

____

____

____

____

____

____

____

____

Arrangement diagram:

Services I'd like during my vigil:

- ❏ Massage
- ❏ Reiki
- ❏ Healing Touch
- ❏ Sound Healing
- ❏ Singing bowls
- ❏ Therapeutic Musician
- ❏ Chakra Balancing
- ❏ Aromatherapy
- ❏ Essential oils
- ❏ Acupuncture
- ❏ Guided meditation/ imagery
- ❏ No services
- ❏ **Other (list below):**

Spiritual/ religious rites/ rituals to be performed during my vigil:

____

____

____

____

____

____

____

____

____

____

____

____

Readings:

____

____

____

____

____

____

____

Prayers:

____

____

____

____

____

____

____

Other:

____

____

____

____

____

____

Readings:

____

Is there anything else that you DON'T want to happen during your vigil?

____

____

____

____

____

____

____

____

Other:

____

____

____

____

____

____

____

____

____

<u>**At The Time Of My Death**</u>

Are there any religious/spiritual/ceremonial rites/rituals that should be performed?

____

____

____

____

____

____

____

Readings:

____

____

____

____

____

____

____

Prayers:

____

____

____

____

____

Prayers continued:

____

____

____

Other:

____

____

____

____

____

____

____

____

____

____

Would you like your body to be washed and anointed? Who will care for your body in the process?

____

____

____

____

Would you like to be dressed or placed in a shroud? If dressed, what would you like to wear?

____

____

____

____

____

____

When should family and friends be notified of your passing?

____

____

____

____

____

Who is responsible for contacting friends and family? List contact information:

____

____

____

____

____

____

How long would you like your body to remain in the vigil location after death? Would you like viewing and visitations during this time?

____

____

____

____

____

____

If your body will be transported to a funeral home, what is the name, address and phone number of the facilities you'd like to use?

____

____

____

____

____

Is there anything else that you DON'T want at the time of your passing?

<u>My Disposition Wishes</u>

Person(s) responsible for carrying out my disposition plan and their contact information:

If you plan to use a funeral home, what is the name, address and phone number of the facilities you'd like to use?

If you plan to have a home viewing, visitation and funeral, what is the address of the location and who is the person to contact?

Are you an organ donor? ____

Views regarding autopsy?____

Religious/spiritual views to be accounted for:

Disposition options (laws and options vary in each state):

- ❏ **Green burial**
- ❏ **Traditional burial**
- ❏ **Burial at sea**
- ❏ **Traditional cremation**
- ❏ **Direct cremation**
- ❏ **Water cremation** (Alkaline hydrolysis. Legal in Oregon, Missouri, Minnesota, Maryland, Maine, Kansas, Illinois, Florida, Colorado, Georgia, Wyoming, Idaho, Nevada, California, and Utah.)
- ❏ **Embalming** (not legally required in any state, may be required for public viewing at funeral homes or under other circumstances.)
- ❏ **Body donation**
- ❏ **Recomposition** (**Legal in** Washington State)
- ❏ **Mausoleum**

Organization, addresses, contact information related to disposition options:

Options for Cremains (check all that apply. You can use numbers to order preference):

- ❏ Burial
- ❏ To be kept at a loved ones home in an urn/container
- ❏ To be shared in miniature urns/containers between family/friends
- ❏ Scattered (land, sea, air)
- ❏ Sent to outer space
- ❏ Jewelry
- ❏ Columbarium
- ❏ Coral Reef
- ❏ Memorial Tattoos
- ❏ Fireworks
- ❏ Bio urn (Trees, ice floats, etc.)
- ❏ Vinyl Records
- ❏ Painting or other artwork
- ❏ Ceramics, pottery.
- ❏ Other

Additional details or contact information for cremains (organizations, people to contact, etc.)

If burial is to take place, list the address and contact information for the cemetery or burial location:

What clothing would you like to be buried in? Include jewelry and accessories.

____

____

____

____

Hair, make-up, manicure preferences:

____

____

____

____

Facial hair preferences:

____

____

____

____

Are there any items that you'd like to be buried with?

____

____

____

____

____

Describe your ideal burial container (Casket/coffin,box, urn. etc) What materials, fittings, colors would you like?

____

____

____

____

____

If you would like a headstone or grave marker, describe it below. Include materials, size, photos, artwork, etc.)

____

____

____

____

____

____

____

What should be written on your headstone/grave marker. (Names, dates, epitaph, poems, religious/spiritual scripture, etc.)

____

____

____

____

____

____

____

Is there anything else that you DON'T want regarding disposition?

____

____

____

____

____

____

____

<u>My Obituary Wishes</u>

- ❏ **I <u>do not</u> want an obituary published in the newspaper.**
- ❏ **I would like my obituary published in the newspaper.**
- ❏ **I would like my obituary to be published on the funeral home website.**
- ❏ **I have composed my own obituary.**

  Location of my completed obituary:

Person responsible for writing my obituary and their contact information:

I would like the following information included in my obituary (see My Personal Contact Information & Details on page 2.)

❏ My maiden name	❏ Cause of death
❏ My nickname(s)	❏ Death date
❏ Birthday	❏ Places lived
❏ Age	❏ Occupation(s)
❏ Wedding anniversary date	❏ Education
❏ Or, number of years married/together	❏ Military Service
	❏ Religious/Spiritual Affiliations
❏ Place of birth	❏ Membership of organizations and clubs
❏ Citizenship	

- ❏ **Include information for donations to organizations (note specific details below):**

❑ **The following family members should be mentioned by name:**

- ❑ My partner/spouse
- ❑ Former partner/spouse
- ❑ My children and their partners
- ❑ My grandchildren
- ❑ My great-grandchildren
- ❑ My siblings

❑ **The following people should also be mentioned by name:**

❑ **Pets that should be mentioned:**

❑ **Please include some of my favorite things and pastimes in my obituary (list items below):**

Other information to be included in my obituary:

Is there anything else that you DON'T want to be included in your obituary?

<u>**My Viewing and Visitation Wishes**</u>

Person(s) responsible for carrying out my viewing/visitation plan and their contact information:

____

____

____

____

____

____

Where will the visitation/viewing be held?

____

____

____

____

____

Do you have a preference for day/time for the visitation? How long should it last?

____

____

____

Should there be a guestbook or memory book?

____

____

____

Would you like flowers?

____

____

____

____

Are there any spiritual/religious rites/rituals or ceremonies that should be held during the visitation/viewing?

____

____

____

____

____

Readings or prayers during the visitation:

____

____

____

____

____

____

If you will have a casket/coffin, do you want it open or closed? (depending on the circumstances of your death.)

____

____

____

____

____

____

If you're a verteran, do you want military services?

____

____

____

____

____

____

Music to be played:

Music that should not be played:

Musician(s) and contact information:

May family and friends include items they'd like to have buried with you?

____

____

____

Items that should be present at the visitation/viewing but not buried with me:

____

____

____

____

____

____

Other visitation/viewing wishes:

____

____

____

____

____

____

____

____

____

____

____

Is there anything else that you DON'T want to happen viewing/visitation?

____

____

____

____

____

<h1 style="text-align:center"><u>My Funeral/ Memorial Wishes</u></h1>

Person(s) responsible for carrying out my funeral/memorial plan and their contact information:

____

____

____

____

____

____

Where will the funeral be held?

____

____

____

____

____

Do you have a preference for the day/time of your funeral ?

____

____

____

Should there be a guestbook or memory book?

____

____

____

Would you like flowers?

____

____

____

____

Are there any spiritual/religious rites/rituals or ceremonies that should be held during the funeral?

____

____

____

____

____

____

____

____

____

____

Readings or prayers during the funeral:

____

____

____

____

____

____

____

____

____

____

Music to be played:

____

____

____

____

____

____

Music that should not be played:

____

____

____

____

____

____

Musician(s) and contact information:

____

____

____

____

____

If you will have a casket/coffin, who will be the pallbearers and what is their contact information? Choose 6 people who can carry at least 60 lbs.

____

____

____

____

____

____

Would you like honorary pallbearers? List contact information. 1-2 people.

____

____

Would you like an officiant or another individual(s) to speak at your funeral?

____

____

____

____

Do you want a gathering/reception to immediately follow the funeral such as a luncheon?

____

____

____

____

Person(s) responsible for organizing this gathering and their contact information:

____

____

____

____

____

Location and address of after reception:

____

____

____

____

Foods to be served:

____

____

____

____

____

____

Memorial Activities:

____

____

____

____

____

____

Other wishes:

____

____

____

____

____

____

____

____

____

____

____

Is there anything else that you DON'T want to happen during your funeral?

____

____

____

____

____

____

____

____

____

<u>My Legacy Projects and Wishes</u>

I have completed the following Legacy projects. Listed below are where they can be found and other instructions regarding the projects:

I would like for family and friends to honor my legacy by doing the following things (celebrating birthday/ deathday, donations, starting a foundation, art projects, legacy projects, etc):

Is there anything else that you DON'T want family/friends to do to honor you?

____

____

____

44

____

____

____

____

____

____

____

Executor of my Will or person(s) responsible regarding my finances and their contact information:

____

____

____

____

____

List any insurance policies or account information for arrangement expenses:

____

____

____

____

____

____

____

____

____

____

____

____

____

____

____

____

____

<h1 style="text-align:center"><u>Other Information</u></h1>

In this section, include any other information or details not previously covered.